STECK-VAUGHN BOLDPRINT®

Wild World of Sports

ADELE SAMUEL

HOUGHTON MIFFLIN HARCOURT

10801 N. Mopac Expressway
Building # 3
Austin, TX 78759
1.800.531.5015

Steck-Vaughn is a trademark of HMH Supplemental Publishers Inc. registered in the United States of America and/or other jurisdictions. All inquiries should be mailed to HMH Supplemental Publishers Inc., P.O. Box 27010, Austin, TX 78755.

www.rubiconpublishing.com

Associate Publisher: Miriam Bardswich
Editor: Dawna McKinnon
Creative/Art Director: Jennifer Drew
Designer: Waseem Bashar
Cover–© Flirt / SuperStock; Title Page Image–Shutterstock

Printed in Singapore

ISBN: 978-1-4190-4020-7
8 9 10 11 12 13 14 15 16 17 2016 24 23 22 21 20 19 18 17 16 15
A B C D E F G

CONTENTS

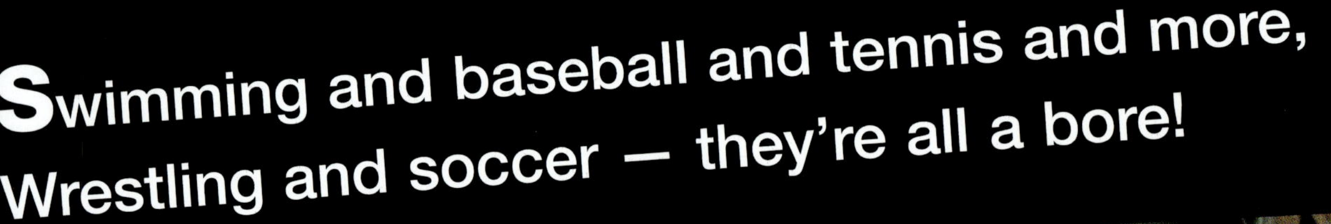

Swimming and baseball and tennis and more,
Wrestling and soccer — they're all a bore!

In winter you might play ice hockey or ski,
But they're not for everyone, don't you agree?

If you're ready to check out strange games of all sorts,
Be sure to enter the ***Wild World of Sports!***

10 REASONS BASEBALL Is a WEIRD SPORT

warm up

Are there any rules in sports that you think are strange? Make a list and compare your list with a partner's.

If a batter fails two-thirds of the time, he or she is still considered an excellent batter. …

It is legal to "steal" in this game. …

CHECKPOINT

What does "steal" mean here?

If you aren't such a good hitter, you can have a pinch hitter bat for you. If you aren't such a fast runner, you can have someone — a pinch runner — come in and run for you. …

There's a rule preventing pitchers from spitting on the ball. They can spit anywhere else they like, apparently.

If a batter walks with the bases loaded, he or she is credited with an RBI (Run Batted In). That's right: even though he or she didn't hit the ball.

The game is played on dirt and grass, but if the ball gets dirty, it is replaced with a new, clean ball.

If a batter accidentally hits the catcher when swinging, it's the catcher's fault, even if the catcher gets injured. The batter is awarded a base. The catcher gets an apology, if he or she is lucky.

The coaches and managers wear the same uniforms as the players.

When a pitcher *walks* a batter, the batter *jogs* to first base. …

The seventh-inning stretch makes baseball the only sport where spectators must take part in calisthenics.

calisthenics: *exercises*

wrap up

1. Choose one of the reasons why baseball is weird and write a journal entry explaining it.
2. With a partner, discuss whether or not you think rule #1 should be applied to other things in life. What things? When?
3. In a small group, choose another popular sport and try to make up your own list of reasons it is weird.

Baseball field, ball–Shutterstock

YOU CALL THAT A SPORT?

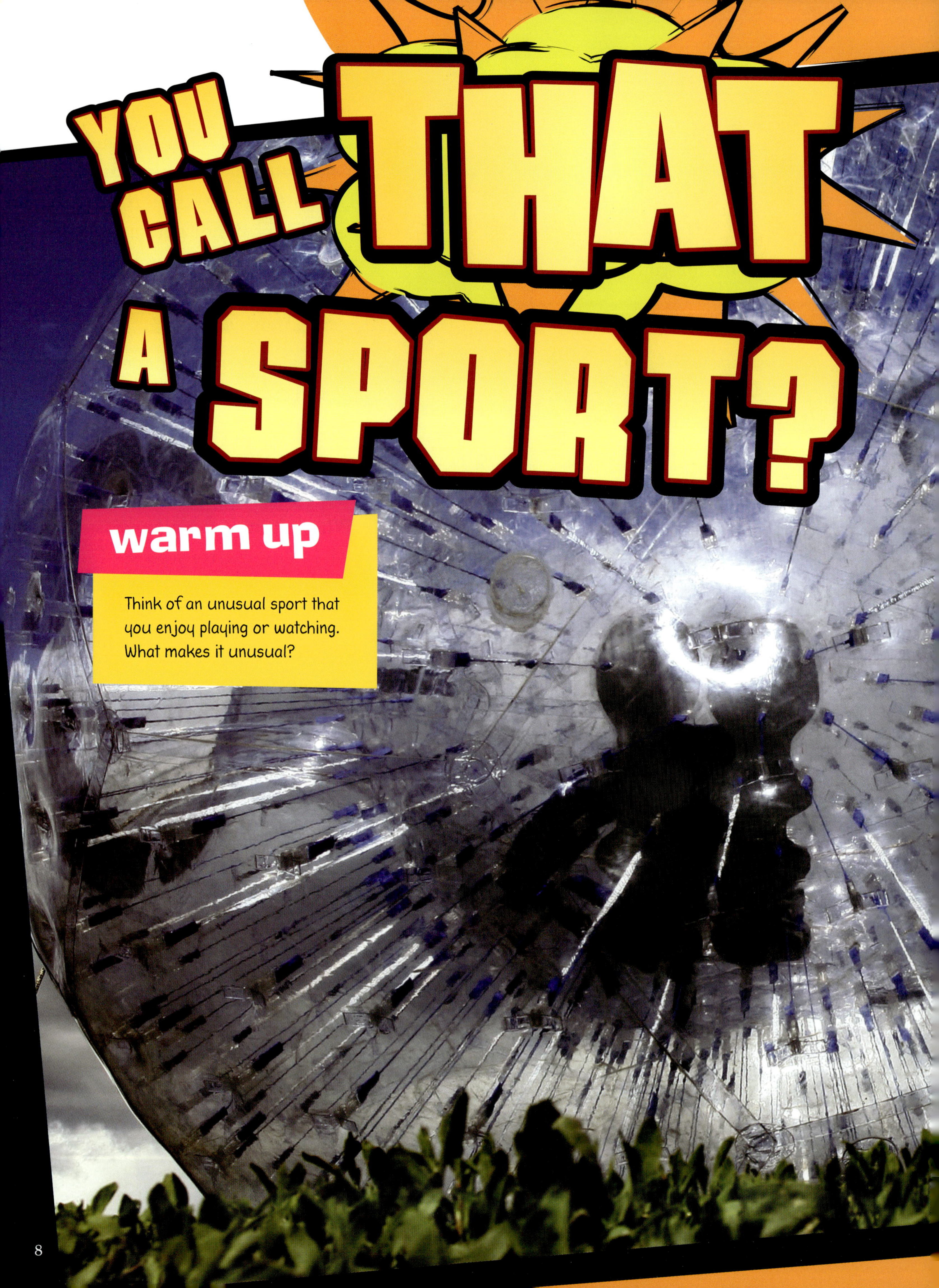

warm up

Think of an unusual sport that you enjoy playing or watching. What makes it unusual?

Do you think zorbing is something aliens do? Do you think underwater hockey is something mermaids might play? If so, BOLDPRINT is here to help. Here's a list of some of the most unique sports around.

unique: *different; unusual*

ZORBING

Zorbing started in New Zealand. In dry zorbing, a person is strapped inside a big inflated ball, pushed over the top of a hill, and left to bounce and roll down to the bottom. The steeper the hill, the better the ride!

In wet zorbing, or liquid zorbing, participants aren't strapped in and have to run like hamsters on wheels. Add some soapy water inside the ball and you have a recipe for a wild ride!

inflated: *filled with air or gas*

UNDERWATER HOCKEY

Like its on-ice relative, underwater hockey involves one team trying to put a puck in another team's net. The only difference — it's at the bottom of a pool! Players use short sticks that can easily be used with one hand to control a puck. But it's not as easy as it seems. Underwater hockey requires some protective equipment. Players wear thick gloves on their hands to protect them from the bottom of the pool.

They also wear water caps and mouth guards. A game consists of two 15-minute halves with a three-minute halftime.

CHECKPOINT

Why do you think the stick would be used with one hand?

MOUNTAIN UNICYCLING

Imagine riding down a steep hill on a bike with only one wheel and no handlebars! Mountain cyclists looking for a greater challenge are trading in their bikes for unicycles. Balance, steering, and braking are much more difficult on a unicycle because you can't use your hands. Add some rocky terrain or snow and you've got quite a ride!

terrain: *surface of land*

Mountain unicycling– Aurora/Getty Images; bossaball–Courtesy of Bossaball Ltd./Filip Eyckmans

BOSSABALL

If you enjoy bouncing around, this is a sport for you! Bossaball is a variation of a few different sports – mainly volleyball, soccer, and gymnastics. It involves an inflatable court, which is divided by a net. Both sides of the net include a trampoline. The object of the game is to hit the ball to the ground of the opponent's side. In bossaball, players can use any part of their bodies to hit the ball. If that doesn't sound fun enough, add in some samba! Players play to music, and referees might even carry instruments. It's a very important part of the game.

FREE DIVING

What's so unusual about diving, you ask? How about diving without a tank! In free diving, divers hold their breath while diving into deep water. To help them get to these great depths, divers hold on to a weighted sled that is attached to a line. The sled pulls them down. When they can't hold their breath any longer, a floating device brings them back to the surface. Divers often compete to see who can hold their breath the longest.

device: *piece of equipment*

FYI

The world record for free diving is held by Herbert Nitsch of Austria. On October 2, 2005, he dived to a depth of 564 feet, all in a single breath!

Free diving–istockphoto; Extreme ironing–Photo by Crazy Chameleon/eyevine/KPA-ZUMA/KEYSTONE Press

EXTREME IRONING

Ever wished you could climb a mountaintop and iron your favorite shirt? If so, extreme ironing is the sport for you! This sport (there seems to be much debate on whether or not this is a sport) is reported to have been invented in 1997 by Phil Shaw of England, who had chores to do but wanted to go rock climbing instead. He decided to do both, and the sport was born.

Since then, extreme ironing has been performed on cliffs, mountaintops, in canoes, underwater, on top of landmarks and buildings, and while skiing and snowboarding. It just goes to show that any chore can be fun if you use your imagination!

CHECKPOINT

Why do you think there is debate about whether extreme ironing is a sport?

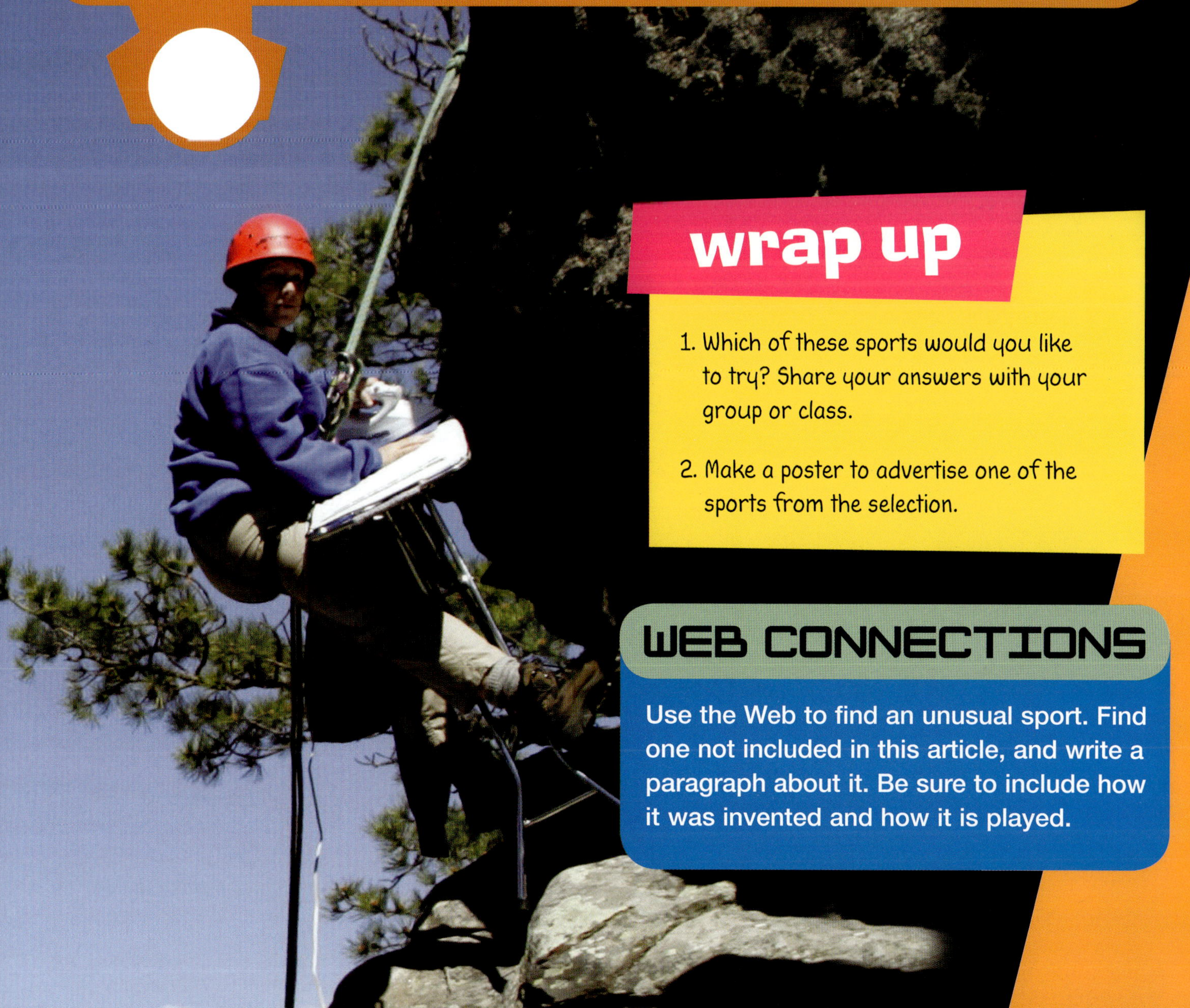

wrap up

1. Which of these sports would you like to try? Share your answers with your group or class.

2. Make a poster to advertise one of the sports from the selection.

WEB CONNECTIONS

Use the Web to find an unusual sport. Find one not included in this article, and write a paragraph about it. Be sure to include how it was invented and how it is played.

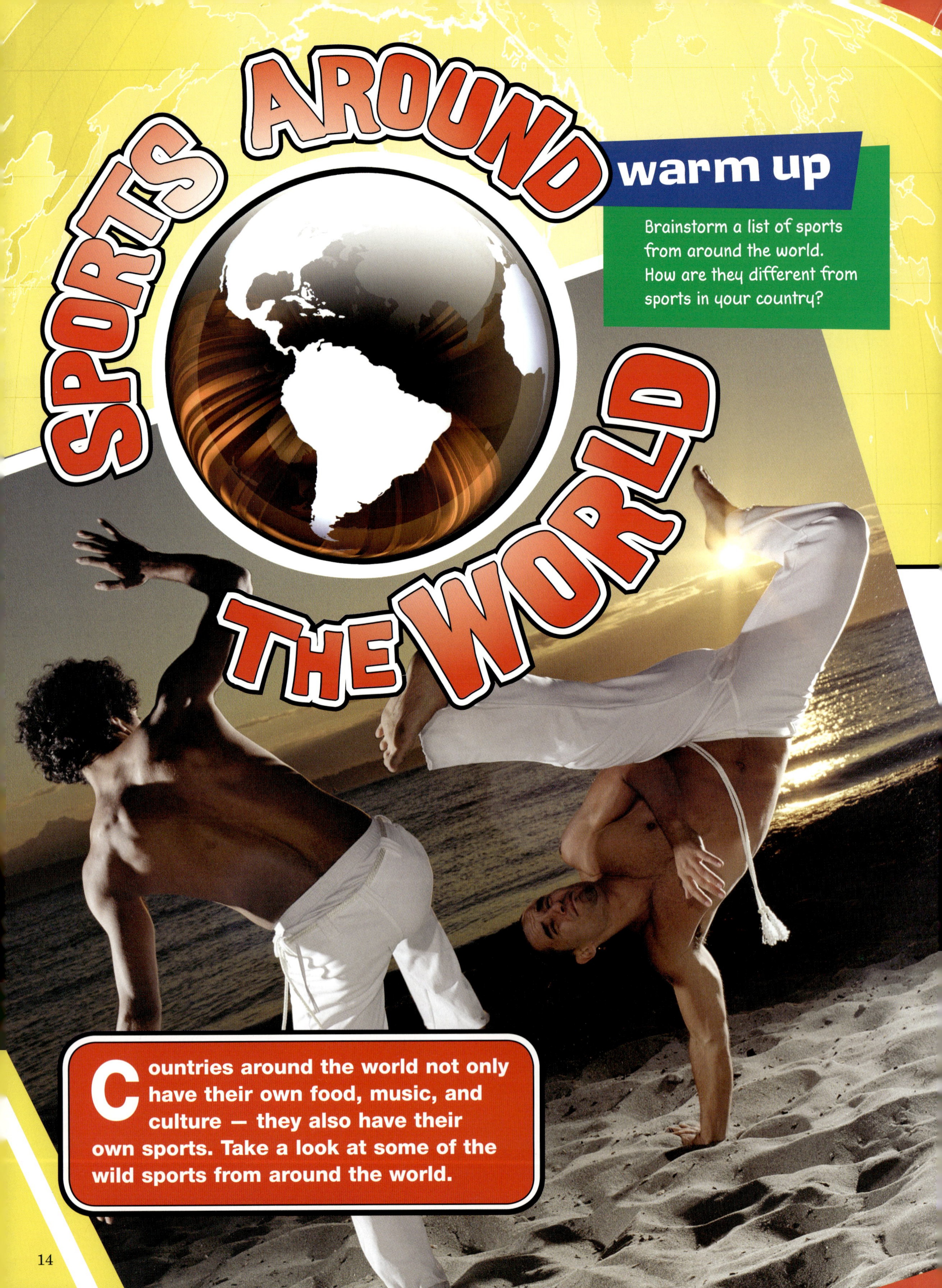

SPORTS AROUND THE WORLD

warm up

Brainstorm a list of sports from around the world. How are they different from sports in your country?

Countries around the world not only have their own food, music, and culture — they also have their own sports. Take a look at some of the wild sports from around the world.

ELEPHANT POLO

THAILAND, NEPAL, SRI LANKA

- It is similar to polo, but elephants are used instead of horses.
- Each elephant carries a trainer called a mahout.
- The mahouts push behind the elephants' ears with their feet to steer them.
- Soccer balls were once used, but the elephants liked smashing them! Now standard polo balls are used.

CAPOERIA

BRAZIL

- It combines dance, music, and acrobatics with martial arts moves.
- It is an Afro-Brazilian martial art developed originally by African slaves. Slaves convinced their owners that they were practicing ritual dances, when they were really developing fighting skills.

CHECKPOINT

Why do you think the slaves wanted their owners to think they were dancing?

- It uses kicks, sweeps, and head-butts. It can go from graceful dance-like movements to deadly fighting in an instant.

---

ritual: *performed according to past customs*

CHINLONE

MYANMAR

- Six players pass a wicker ball in a circle with their feet and knees. If the ball hits the ground, the play must start again.
- It is a combination of sport and dance. The goal is to pass the ball beautifully.
- It is more than 1,500 years old.
- All passes go through a player who dances in the middle.

Capoeria–The Image Bank/Getty Images; elephant polo–Yuttasak Jannarong/Shutterstock.com; all other images Shutterstock

HURLING

IRELAND

- The object of the game is to carry the sliotar (ball) down the field and score on the opposing team's net — sort of like hockey.
- The earliest games were between villages and ended when one team forced the ball over the town line. Games lasted for days and were violent and bloody!

The Gaelic sport of hurling is said to be the ancient ancestor of many sports, including soccer and hockey.

SKIJORING

SCANDINAVIA

- Skiers are towed by horses or dogs attached to harnesses.
- It combines cross-country skiing and dog sledding.
- Skijoring can be done alone or as part of a race.

COMBINE DEMOLITION DERBY

THE UNITED STATES AND CANADA

- People drive old combines and try to hit each other.
- Combine Demolition Derbies take place in farming communities in the prairies, where old farm machinery is as plentiful as pickup trucks.
- Riders stay safe by removing the truck's glass and relocating the gas tank.
- The last combine moving wins!

CHECKPOINT

Why do you think there are so many pickup trucks?

wrap up

With a partner or two, make up a trivia game based on the facts in this article and facts about other sports you know. Play the game with others in your group or class.

WEB CONNECTIONS

Choose one of the sports mentioned in this article. Use the Web to find out the rules of the sport.

Hurling–Getty Images; skijoring–AP/ Daily Interlake / Robin Loznak; combine demolition–AP / East Liverpool Review / Wayne Maris

YOU DID WHAT?

WEIRD SPORTS RECORDS

warm up

In a small group, brainstorm sports records that you know. Do you know any records for unusual sports?

Underwater juggling—AP / Vincent Thian; all other images—Shutterstock

Extreme Ironing Underwater

Yes, you read correctly. In Geelong, Australia, 70 members of the Bay City Scuba Diving Club ironed underwater at the same time. They used cold, non-electric irons to help raise more than $600 for a charity.

CHECKPOINT
In what other places could you do extreme ironing?

Largest Pillow Fight

In April 2005, the University of Albany in New York became a battle zone — for pillows, that is — when 3,648 students unleashed their exam stress in the biggest pillow fight ever.

Longest Underwater Juggling

Ashrita Furman holds the record for the most Guinness World Records. One of his records involved juggling underwater with three balls for 48 minutes and 36 seconds.

CHECKPOINT
Think about how difficult it would be to throw and catch underwater.

Greatest Toe Wrestler

Between 1994 and 2002, Alan Nash of the United Kingdom won five World Championship titles for wrestling with his big toe. What a feat!

Zorbing Record

If you've ever watched a hamster running on its wheel and thought it looked like fun, here's a record for you! Rich Eley rolled a total of 1,059 feet and reached a speed of 31 miles per hour.

Largest Bungee Jump on the Same Rope

What's better than falling through the air alone? Falling through the air with 31 friends! In 2000, 31 thrill-seekers plunged 213 feet together on one bungee rope in Flensburg, Germany.

Fastest Wife Carrier

Wife carrying (which is exactly as it sounds) originated in Finland. In July 2000, Birgit Ulricht carried Margo Uusorg through a 770-foot obstacle course in 55.5 seconds. A service fit for a queen!

Farthest 24-Hour Bathtub Sail

In 1983, 13 prison officers from England set sail in a bathtub for 24 hours straight. By the end of the race, they had traveled a total of 90 miles. Ahoy!

wrap up

1. With a partner, create your own weird sports record. Remember, the more unusual the better.
2. Which records are the most unusual? Rank them in order from most to least unusual. Compare your rankings with a partner's.

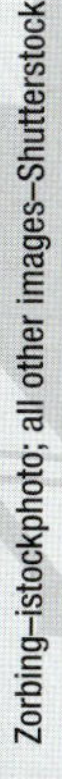

Zorbing–istockphoto; all other images–Shutterstock

THE PERFECT

By Neal Levin

warm up

What do you think the perfect sport is? Share your answer with a partner.

SPORT

I THINK I'VE FOUND THE PERFECT SPORT.
YES, SIR, I'M PRETTY CERTAIN.
NO CHANGING IN THE LOCKER ROOM.
NO FLIMSY SHOWER CURTAIN. ...

NO BIGGER BULLIES ACTING TOUGH.
NO PUNCHING AND NO FIGHTING.
NO NAME-CALLING, NO NASTY WORDS.
NO HAIR PULLING, NO BITING.

NO PARENTS HAVING ARGUMENTS.
NO GRUNTS OR GROANS OR MOANS.
NO BRUISES AND NO BANDAGES.
NO FRACTURED, BROKEN BONES. ...

NO BROKENHEARTED CRYBABIES.
NO WHINING AND NO WEEPING.
YES, SIR, I'VE FOUND THE PERFECT SPORT.
THE PERFECT SPORT IS SLEEPING.

wrap up

1. Reread the poem. Choose what you think are the five worst things that happen in regular sports. Rank these from 1-5, with #1 being the very worst thing.
2. With a partner, brainstorm characteristics of another perfect sport. Share these with your group or class.

Sleeping–Taxi/Getty Images

Adventure on Ice

THE LAKE WAS AS SMOOTH AS GLASS AND THE WIND WAS BLOWING. IT WAS A PERFECT DAY FOR ICEBOATING.

WOW, LOOK AT THE LAKE!

THE WINDSTORM LAST NIGHT REALLY CLEARED AWAY A LOT OF SNOW.

LET'S GO ICEBOATING!

HEY GUYS, DON'T FORGET YOU HAVE TO SHOVEL MR. BHOT'S DRIVEWAY.

Illustrated by Mike Rooth

WE'LL SHOVEL HERE FOR A BIT, AND THEN WE'LL SNEAK DOWN TO THE LAKE!
COOL!

WHEN THEY WERE DONE AT MR. BHOT'S, THEY PUSHED THEIR ICEBOAT ONTO THE ICE.

THIS IS *SWEET!*
I DON'T THINK I'VE EVER GONE THIS FAST BEFORE. *HOLD ON!*

HEY, WE SHOULD TURN BACK BEFORE DAD COMES HOME.
YEAH, LET'S CROSS THE LAKE AND GO BACK ON THE OTHER SIDE.
DOUG —WHAT'S THAT UP AHEAD?
I THINK IT MIGHT BE OPEN WATER — I ... I CAN'T REALLY TELL BECAUSE OF THE SUN!
OH, NO!

TURN! PULL! PULL!
I'M PULLING! I CAN'T SEE ANYTHING!
CRACK!
WHAT ARE WE GONNA DO?
DAD'S GONNA KILL US!
HE MAY NOT HAVE TO!
ONE OF US HAS TO GET OUT AND PUSH!
IF WE STAND ON THE ICE, WE'LL GO THROUGH FOR SURE!
IF I CAN SLIDE OUT ON MY STOMACH, MAYBE I CAN PUSH IT ...

wrap up

1. Why do you think Ted had to slide on his stomach when he got out of the boat? Explain in one or two sentences.
2. Write an iceboating safety manual for iceboaters like Ted and Doug.

WEB CONNECTIONS

Iceboating was invented by adapting sailboats to ski across ice. Use a search engine to find out what other winter sports were inspired by summer sports.

GOING FOR GOLD

DISCONTINUED OLYMPIC SPORTS

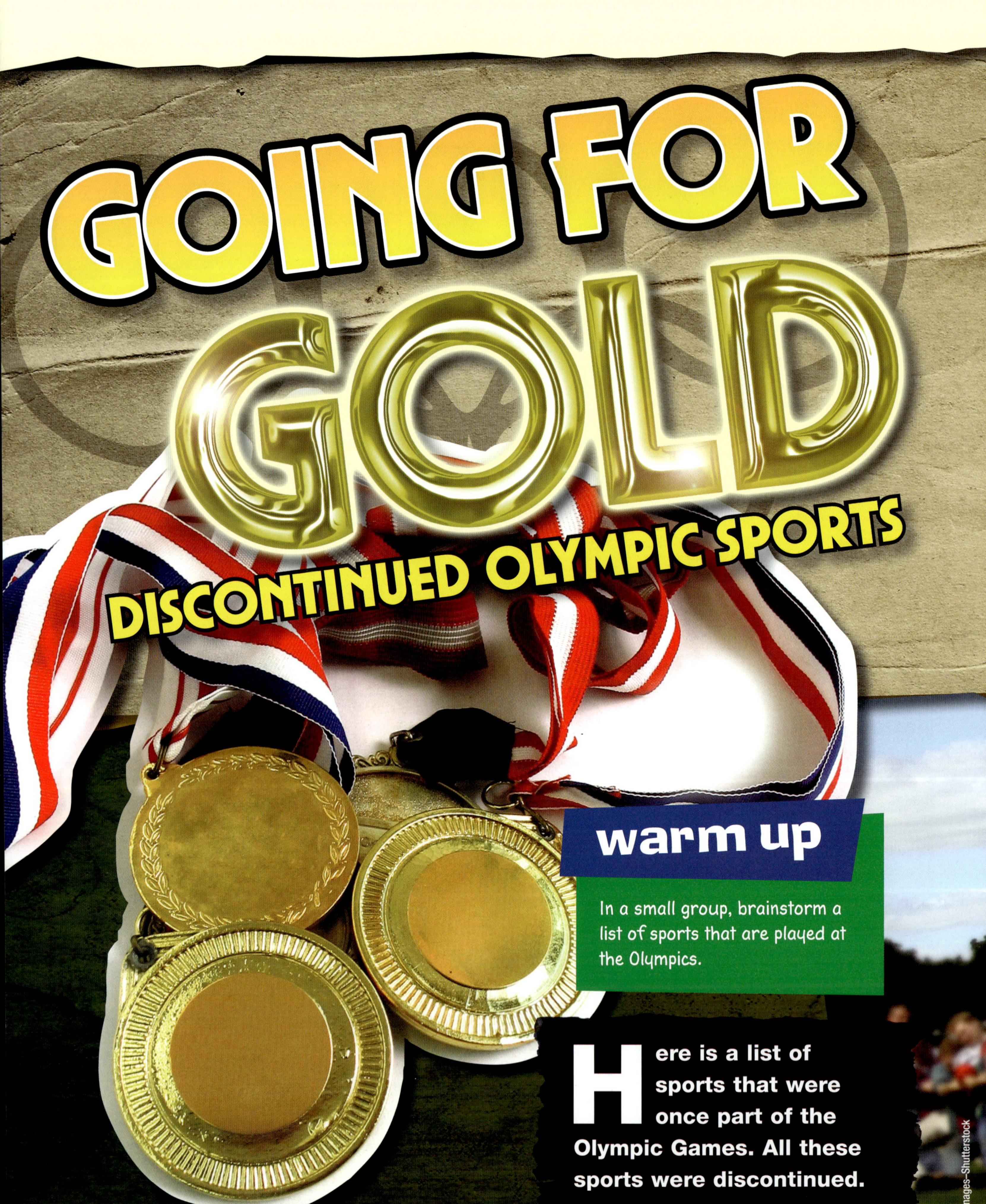

warm up

In a small group, brainstorm a list of sports that are played at the Olympics.

Here is a list of sports that were once part of the Olympic Games. All these sports were discontinued.

All images–Shutterstock

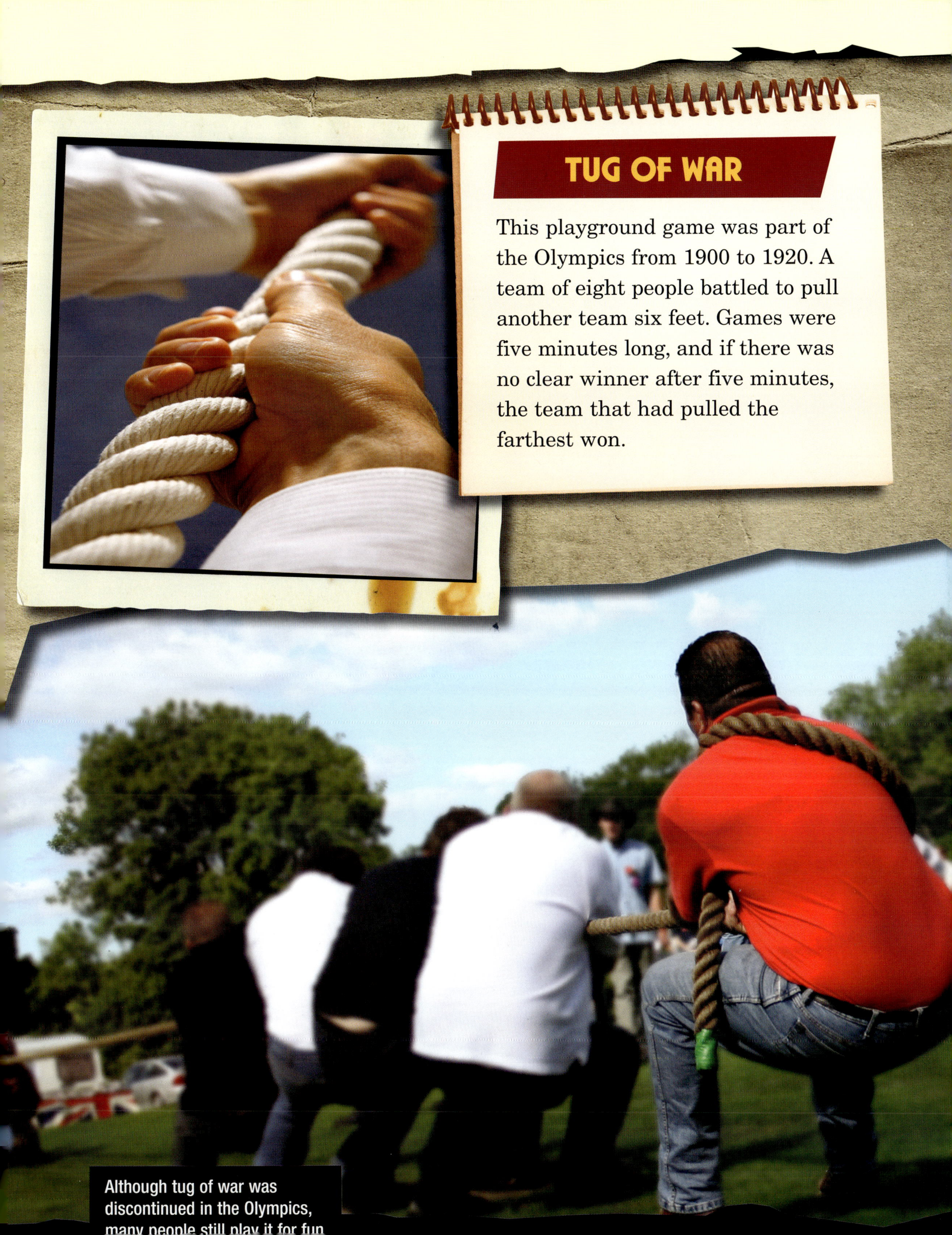

TUG OF WAR

This playground game was part of the Olympics from 1900 to 1920. A team of eight people battled to pull another team six feet. Games were five minutes long, and if there was no clear winner after five minutes, the team that had pulled the farthest won.

Although tug of war was discontinued in the Olympics, many people still play it for fun

LIVE PIGEON SHOOTING

This sport was held only once — in Paris in 1900. Live birds were released for players to shoot. The person who shot the most birds was the winner. As you can imagine, there were dead and injured birds everywhere, and it's reported that the people watching got showered with them. Animal rights groups and the media were very angry, and the event was never held again.

FYI

Live pigeon shooting was banned in most areas shortly after the 1900 Olympics.

SWIMMING OBSTACLE RACE

Another one-hit Olympic wonder from 1900 is the swimming obstacle race. All swimming events were held in the polluted and, at times, fast-running Seine River. The course was 656 feet long, and competitors had to climb over a pole, scramble over a row of boats, and then swim under another row of boats. Frederick Lane of Australia was the Olympic winner, world-record holder, and unbeaten champion of the event!

Swimmers– Library of Congress, Prints & Photographs Division, [reproduction number, 3c07744u]; all other images–Shutterstock

CROQUET

Croquet is yet another sport staged only once in … you guessed it — Paris. In croquet, you have to use a wooden mallet to hit a wooden ball through a series of wire wickets. The person who does it in the least number of hits wins. Competitors from other countries complained to the Olympic Committee that the French team had an unfair advantage because matches took place in France once a week from June until the middle of August!

CHECKPOINT

Why would this be a problem for people from other countries?

wickets: *hoops through which a ball is hit*

MOTORBOATING

Powerboat racing was held only once, in London in 1908. In three separate events, teams raced five times around an eight nautical mile course. Although several teams started out, only France managed to finish the race because of the strong winds that were blowing. Not exactly ideal conditions! Motorboating was dropped from the Olympics after 1908 when all motorized competitions were removed.

nautical mile: *unit of distance used on water and equal to 6,076 feet*

Motorboat from the early 1900s

wrap up

Choose one sport from this list and write a letter to the International Olympic Committee stating reasons the sport should be brought back.

PLAY IT SAFE

warm up

What safety rules do you follow when you play sports?

Sports are fun, but they can be very dangerous! If you are thinking of trying an unusual outdoor sport, know the dangers involved. Read about the following outdoor sports and how athletes prepare for unsafe situations.

All images–Shutterstock

BACKCOUNTRY SKIING

Backcountry skiing is when people ski on mountain slopes that have not been cleared for skiers and do not have safe trails. The mountains are often so remote that the skiers have to travel there by helicopter!

There are no ski patrollers in the mountains. Skiers may get sick or injure themselves on rocks and trees that get in their path.

Staying Safe: Skiers take wilderness first-aid courses to learn how to deal with emergencies. They also never ski alone.

Skiers can get stuck in avalanches, which are large masses of snow, ice, and rock that speed down the mountains.

Staying Safe: Skiers take an avalanche-awareness course and listen to avalanche reports. They always keep safety equipment with them. They bring a shovel for digging and a transmitter, a device that helps others find skiers under snow.

---

remote: *distant; removed*
patrollers: *people who watch out for others*

CAVE DIVING

In cave diving, scuba divers explore dark, mysterious caves located underwater.

Divers easily get lost in caves because they are so dark.

Staying Safe: Responsible divers bring a bright flashlight underwater. They also make a path out of line reel to easily find a way to get out of the cave.

line reel: *flexible type of rope like fishing line*

Sometimes tight cave walls make it hard for divers to move around.

Staying Safe: Divers make sure they take courses to prepare for different cave conditions. They learn how to swim in a horizontal position or dive into a deeper depth of water.

horizontal: *on the same level*

ROCK FISHING

Rock fishing is sea fishing from rocky outcroppings, walls, and cliffs.

outcroppings: *parts of a rock sticking out of the ground*

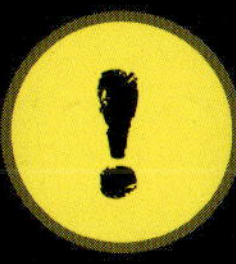

Rising tides, which are waves that last for a long time, can knock fishers down.

Staying Safe: Fishers listen to updated weather news before they go fishing. They also watch the waves and wind to see whether or not the conditions are good.

Water crashes up against rocks and the rocks become slippery.

Staying Safe: Rock fishers wear strong waterproof boots with cleats. They also wear lifejackets and helmets in case they fall into the water. Rock fishers also make sure they never go fishing by themselves.

cleats: *pieces attached to the soles of boots that help hold someone in a steady position*

wrap up

1. Choose one of the sports listed in this article and make a safety poster for it. Share it with your friends.
2. Work with a partner to create a new piece of safety equipment for one of these sports. Draw a picture of your new equipment and explain it to your class.

All images–Shutterstock

CREATE YOUR OWN UNIQUE SPORT

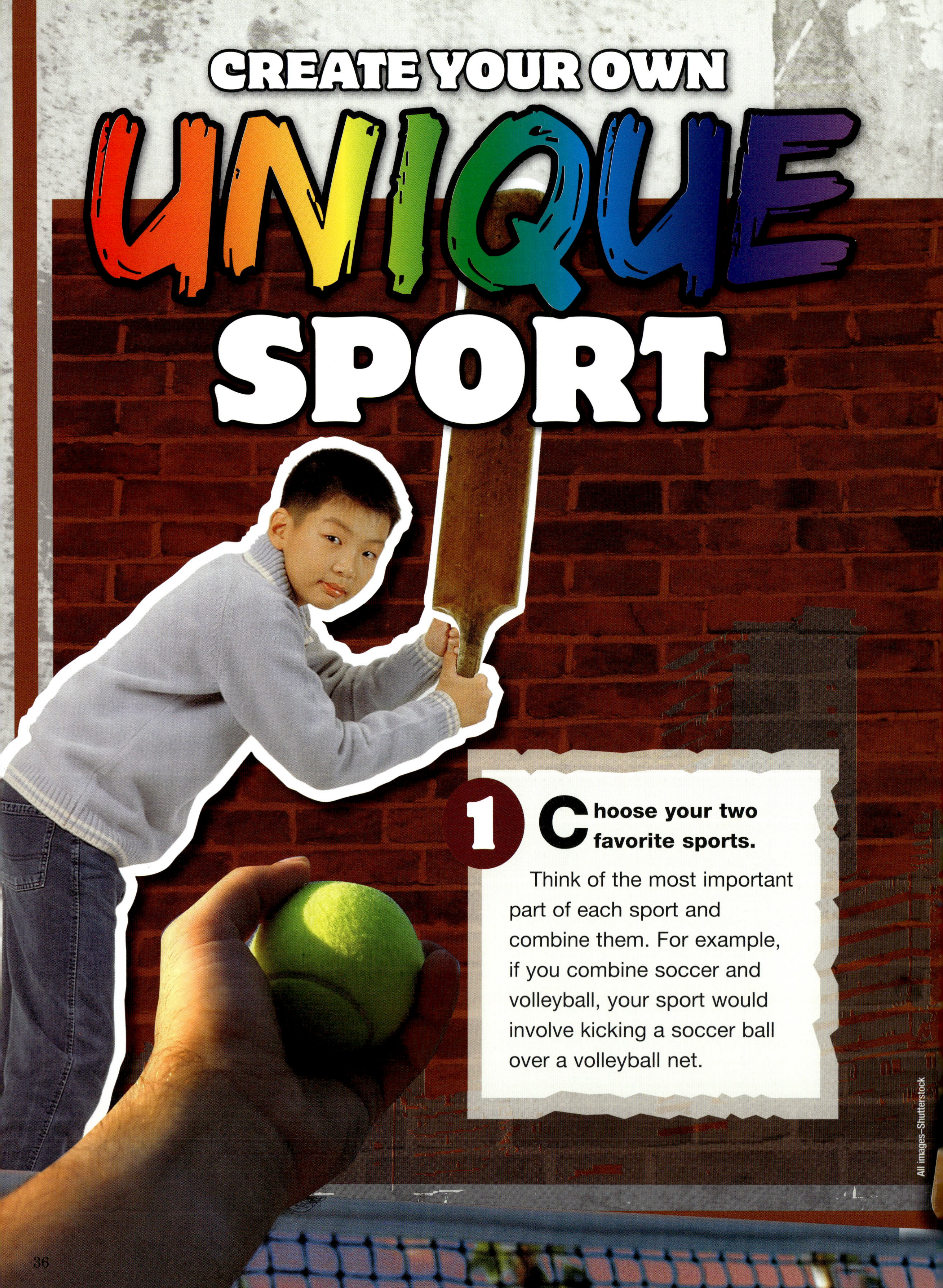

1 Choose your two favorite sports.

Think of the most important part of each sport and combine them. For example, if you combine soccer and volleyball, your sport would involve kicking a soccer ball over a volleyball net.

All images–Shutterstock

2 Make up some rules for your new sport. What is allowed and what is not allowed? Will your sport have rules about what parts of the body can be used? What will be the penalty for breaking the rules? How many points will be awarded? Will there be points? How will the winner be decided? Make an Official Rules Handbook that includes all of the information about your game.

3 Play your new game with a friend or a group of friends. Change any rules that are confusing or don't make sense as you go along. All sports change over time!

4 Think up a great name for your new sport. You can either combine the names of your two original sports, or make up something totally new and imaginative. You can even try looking up the words in other languages.

5 Make up some fake history for your sport to make it sound important. A fake world champion is a must!

6 Create a flyer to advertise your sport.

7 **HAVE FUN!**

THE ULTIMATE

warm up

What games do you play in gym class and at recess?

"Hurry," yelled Tariq. "The bus is coming." Kevin quickly gathered his books and his lunch. He stomped out the door and down the sidewalk to where Tariq was waiting impatiently. "Did you get your homework done?"

"Yeah," said Kevin, "but I don't see the point. It doesn't matter what we write to the parent council. There's no way the school can get any playground equipment this year. It's just a waste of time."

"It's not a waste," said Lorna, who sat down in front of Kevin and Tariq. "It's a new school, and the parent council wants to know what kind of a playground we want. I think it's a cool assignment."

"Lorna's right, Kevin," Tariq replied. "It's really not that bad. We're lucky to go to a new school, and when we get everything, it'll be brand new."

"Yeah, right, no baseball diamond, no basketball hoops, no soccer nets — just a big empty field," said Kevin.

CHECKPOINT

Think about the equipment that you would like to see in a playground.

Later that day they had gym class, which was, or at least used to be, Kevin's favorite subject. Kevin and Tariq changed quickly and met their teacher, Mr. Kim, out on the field.

All images–Shutterstock

GAME

"All right class," called Mr. Kim. "Because we don't have all of our equipment yet, you can have free choice of your activity. There are footballs and jump ropes or you can play four square."

As usual, most of the kids went off to the four-square courts. Kevin sighed. He didn't want to play four square, and jump ropes were for girls. He walked slowly over to the equipment tub to grab a football when he noticed some bright red discs lying in the corner.

"Hey, Mr. Kim. Can Tariq and I play with one of these?" Kevin asked, holding up a disc.

"Sure," replied Mr. Kim. "I didn't even know they were in there."

Kevin and Tariq went out to the field and started tossing the disc.

CHECKPOINT
Do you think this is true? Why or why not?

"This is great," called Kevin.

"Yeah, I haven't played with a disc in a long time," agreed Tariq. Lorna saw the boys playing and ran over to join them, but Kevin and Tariq weren't interested in having a girl play, too. Mr. Kim came over to help solve the problem.

"You know, there is a disc game that you can all play. You don't need any equipment or referees, but boys and girls have to play together. It's called 'ultimate.' Interested?" asked Mr. Kim.

Kevin shuffled his feet while Lorna smiled. "Sure, why not?" she said. "Unless they're worried that I'll beat them."

"The rules are really quite simple," said Mr. Kim. "Ultimate is a bit like football. There are two teams and goal lines just like in football, but there's no tackling. You pass the disc to a teammate and make your way down the field. You need to cross the opposing team's goal line to score a point. The first team to score 10 points wins."

"That's easy," said Tariq. "I'm the fastest in our class. It will be easy for me to score a goal."

"Not so fast," cautioned Mr. Kim. "You're not allowed to run with the disc. Once you catch it, you have to stop and pass it. If you drop the pass, the other team gets the disc."

By now a big group of students huddled around Mr. Kim. "Each team has eight players, four boys and four girls," he continued. Mr. Kim chose two captains, who quickly set up teams. Most of the kids were pretty rusty at first, and the disc went back and forth quickly as each team dropped it.

After a while, however, the students got the hang of the game and before long, play was going fairly smoothly.

"OK, everyone, time to pack it up," called Mr. Kim as the period drew to a close.

"Just five more minutes?" asked Kevin. "We'll change super fast."

"I'm sorry guys. Hit the locker rooms. Social studies starts in 10 minutes."

The rest of the week seemed to drag on. Kevin couldn't wait for the next gym class so that he could play ultimate again. He even used some of the money he had been saving for a new basketball to buy himself a disc. All that week, Kevin took his

disc to school and practiced with Tariq. They let Lorna join in and had to admit that she was pretty good. Word of the game spread quickly, and soon the recess yard was full of flying discs.

Gym class finally arrived. "We have something a little different today," said Mr. Kim. "Mrs. Cochran's class will be joining us."

"Well, everyone, what do you want to play today?" asked Mrs. Cochran. "How about some flag football?"

"Ultimate," cried the kids at the top of their lungs. Each class chose an end and took their positions.

The game started evenly, with the teams trading points back and forth. It was 5 – 0 when Tariq saw Lorna standing halfway down the field. He quickly made a long pass to her, but before she could catch it, Julian, a member of the other team, pushed Lorna down and knocked the disc out of her hands.

"Hey, that was a foul," cried Kevin, running over to help Lorna up. Julian always played rough, and Kevin wasn't about to stand for it.

"No way!" cried Julian. "She just got in my way!" Kevin looked over to the sidelines where Mrs. Cochran and Mr. Kim stood watching. Tariq shouted, "Mr. Kim, Mr. Kim. That was a foul. Didn't you see it?"

"It doesn't matter what I saw," replied Mr. Kim. "There are no referees in this game. You guys have to decide whether it was a foul or not."

CHECKPOINT

This is one of the rules of ultimate. Do you agree with it or not?

Kevin and Julian argued back and forth. Time was ticking away and both teams were anxious to get back to the game. Finally Kevin asked Julian's teammates what they thought, and they agreed that Lorna was already in position when Julian hit her. Julian frowned, but Kevin was smiling. Play resumed from the place where Lorna was hit.

"Next point wins," called out Mr. Kim.

Play started again with Tariq and Kevin passing the disc back and forth. They quickly made their way to the goal line without dropping it. Practice had really paid off.

Tariq was in a position to score. Kevin was about to pass to him, but

---

resumed: *started again*

Julian knew what was coming next and started running to block the pass. At the last second, Kevin changed his strategy, and threw to Lorna, who was wide open. As he threw the disc, a gust of wind came up and blew the disc off course. Everyone held their breath as Lorna made a spectacular dive to make the winning catch. Players on both sides ran to congratulate her.

On the bus ride home that evening, Lorna, Tariq, and Kevin were still buzzing with the excitement of their win. They all decided that ultimate was indeed the ultimate game.

wrap up

1. With a partner, discuss the lessons that Kevin learned playing ultimate.
2. In a small group, complete Kevin's assignment and design a dream playground. List the equipment you would include and draw a sketch of the playground.

RIP-ROARIN' and READY to FLY!

By Kristi Lew

warm up

What two sports do you think kiteboarding combines?

Morgan Skiperdene is barely old enough to drive, but she's already been flying above the waves for five years. This 16-year-old honor student from Cap Hatteras, NC, is one of the best women kiteboarders in the world.

By harnessing the force of the wind, riders like Skiperdene can soar up to 50 feet above the waves.

harnessing: *using*

FYI

Surfboards used for kiteboarding are specially designed for the sport. Larger boards are used for cruising and when there is a light wind. Smaller boards are used for tricks and for speed.

Photos on left page–courtesy of Morgan Skiperdene; kiteboarder–The Image Bank/Getty Images; all other images–Shutterstock

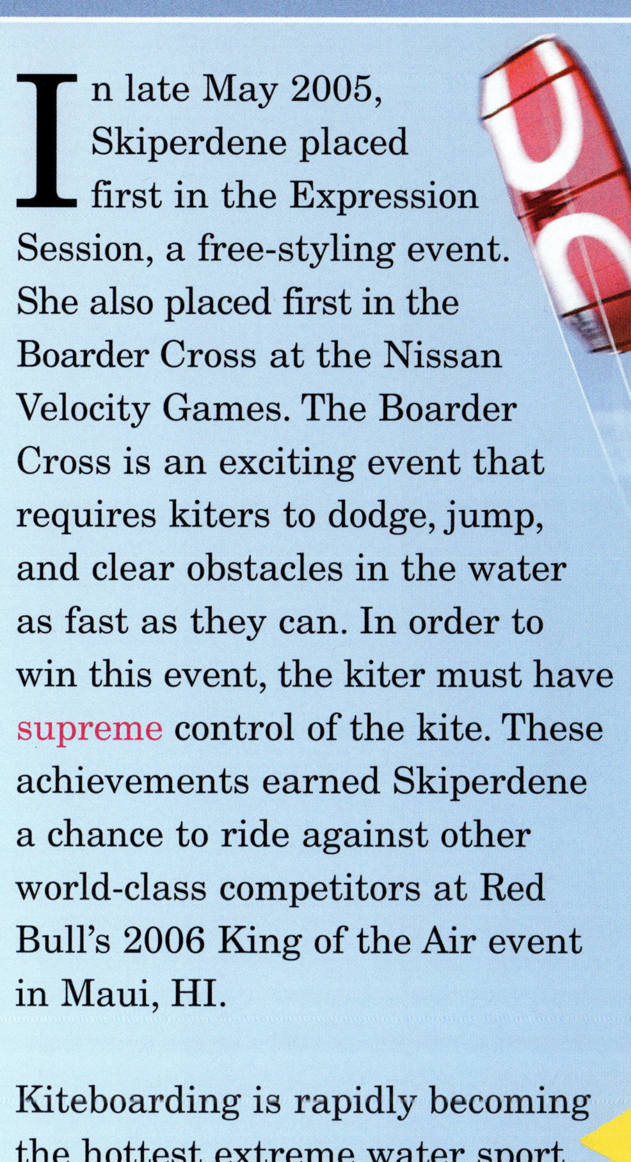

In late May 2005, Skiperdene placed first in the Expression Session, a free-styling event. She also placed first in the Boarder Cross at the Nissan Velocity Games. The Boarder Cross is an exciting event that requires kiters to dodge, jump, and clear obstacles in the water as fast as they can. In order to win this event, the kiter must have supreme control of the kite. These achievements earned Skiperdene a chance to ride against other world-class competitors at Red Bull's 2006 King of the Air event in Maui, HI.

Kiteboarding is rapidly becoming the hottest extreme water sport in the world. It's already wildly popular in the coastal regions of North Carolina, Florida, and Hawaii, and it's beginning to catch on in areas boasting inland lakes and rivers, too. If you're lucky enough to stumble onto a kite beach on a day with good wind, you're likely to see dozens of kiters rocketing off the waves and performing amazing tricks while attached to the fluorescent arcs of their kites.

How exactly do kiters catch so much mad air? Easy — they do it by becoming masters of their kites!

CHECKPOINT
What other extreme sports are hot?

---

supreme: *the best*
boasting: *having and displaying*
fluorescent: *very bright in color*

The Kite

Kiteboarding kites range in size from two square metres [21 square feet] to 22 square metres [236 square feet]. Most experienced kite-boarders have several different-size kites for various wind conditions. The larger the surface area, the more powerful the kite. So bigger kites are reserved for calmer days, and on days when the wind is screaming, the smaller kites come in handy.

A kite acts like a wing. And just like a bird's wing or an airplane wing, a kiter's kite produces lift. Most of the lift comes from the kite's shape ...; the rest comes from drag — the wind hitting below the kite's surface. ...

If you're interested in learning to kiteboard, learning how to fly the kite is key. You start with a specially designed, inexpensive trainer kite. It's too small to pull you off the ground but has the same controls as bigger kiteboarding kites.

---

lift: *upward force caused by the wind*

All images–Shutterstock

According to Chris Moore, an instructor from Kitty Hawk Kites in North Carolina, at least 80 percent of the learning curve in kiteboarding is mastering kite control.

CHECKPOINT

What do you think "learning curve" means?

Morgan Skiperdene agrees. "Learn to control your kite on land first," she advises. "I started flying the kite two years before I even got on the board."

Even though it's not necessary to spend years on land before getting in the water, the fact that Skiperdene was so dedicated to mastering her kite might just be why she has become one of the best kiteboarders around.

wrap up

1. With a partner, discuss how kiteboarding is similar to both surfing and parasailing.
2. Make a poster advertising a kiteboarding event. Share it with your class.

ACKNOWLEDGMENTS

The publisher gratefully acknowledges the following for permission to reprint copyrighted material in this book.

Every reasonable effort has been made to trace the owners of copyrighted material and to make due acknowledgment. Any errors or omissions drawn to our attention will be gladly rectified in future editions.

Neal Levin: "The Perfect Sport." Permission courtesy of Neal Levin.

Excerpt from ODYSSEY's May 2006 issue:
At the Edge: Science of Extreme Sports, © 2006, Carus Publishing Company, published by Cobblestone Publishing, 30 Grove Street, Suite C, Peterborough, NH 03458. All Rights Reserved. Used by permission of the publisher.

"10 Reasons Baseball Is a Weird Sport": Permission courtesy of MSN ENCARTA.